JOHN PHILIP SOUSA
arr. Robert Gower

THE WASHINGTON POST MARCH

MUSIC DEPARTMENT

OXFORD
UNIVERSITY PRESS

The Washington Post March

JOHN PHILIP SOUSA
(1854–1932)
arr. Robert Gower

Printed in Great Britain

OXFORD UNIVERSITY PRESS, MUSIC DEPARTMENT, GREAT CLARENDON STREET, OXFORD OX2 6DP

Con larghezza